The Law Of Attrc
To Abunc

Law Of Attraction

Step-By-Step Guide To Unleash The Power Within Your Subconscious Mind And Get What You Want Through Manifestation!

Ryan Cooper

Copyright © 2014 Ryan Cooper

STOP!!! Before you read any further....Would you like to know the Success Secrets of how to make Passive Income Online?

If your answer is yes, then you are not alone. Thousands of people are looking for the secret to learning how to create their own online passive income style business.

If you have been searching for these answers without much luck, you are in the right place!

Because I want to make sure to give you as much value as possible for purchasing this book, right now for a limited time you can get 3 incredible bonuses for free.

At the end of this book I describe all 3 bonuses. You can access them at the end. But for those of you that want to grab your bonuses right now. See below.

Just Go Here For Free Instant Access:

www.OperationAwesomeLife.com/FreeBonuses

Legal Notice

All rights reserved. Without limiting the rights under the copyright reserved above, no part of this publication may be reproduced, stored in or introduced into a retrieval system, or transmitted, in any form, or by any means (electronic, mechanical, photocopying, recording, or otherwise) without the prior written permission of the copyright owner and publisher of this book. This book is copyright protected. This is for your personal use only. You cannot amend, distribute, sell, use, quote or paraphrase any part or the content within this eBook without the consent of the author or copyright owner. Legal action will be pursued if this is breached.

Disclaimer Notice

Please note the information contained within this document is for educational and entertainment purposes only. Considerable energy and every attempt has been made to provide the most up to date, accurate, relative, reliable, and complete information, but the reader is strongly encouraged to seek professional advice prior to using any of this information contained in this book. The reader understands they are reading and using this information contained herein at their own risk, and in no way will the author, publisher, or any affiliates be held responsible for any damages whatsoever. No warranties of any kind are expressed or implied. Readers acknowledge that the author is not engaging in the rendering of legal, financial, medical, or any other professional advice. By reading this document, the reader agrees that under no circumstances is the author, publisher, or anyone else affiliated with the production, distribution, sale, or any other element of this book responsible for any losses, direct or indirect, which are incurred as a result of the use of information contained within this document, including, but not limited to, -errors, omissions, or inaccuracies. Because of the rate with which conditions change, the author and publisher reserve the right to alter and update the information contained herein on the new conditions whenever they see applicable.

Table Of Contents

Introduction

Chapter 1: What Is The Law Of Attraction?

Chapter 2: Practice Brain-Training Strategies

Chapter 3: The Power Of Mindfulness Meditation

Chapter 4: Channeling The Subconscious Mind And The Positive Vibrations

Chapter 5: How To Use Creative Visualization

Chapter 6: How To Manifest Money And Wealth By Law Of Attraction

Chapter 7: Happiness And Law Of Attraction

Chapter 8: Finding Love With Law Of Attraction

Chapter 9: Steps In Using Law Of Attraction In Daily Life

Chapter 10: Dreaming Big With Law Of Attraction

Conclusion

Preview Of: "Manifestation: Ultimate Manifestation Guide! The Science Of Manifestation Through Neuroplasticity, Brain Training, NLP Techniques, Creative Visualization, Mindfulness Meditation, And More!"

Free Bonus Offer

Introduction

I want to thank you and congratulate you for purchasing the book, *"The Law Of Attraction Secrets To Abundance! - Step by Step Guide To Unleash the Power Within Your Subconscious Mind And Get What You Want Through Manifestation."*

This "Law of Attraction" book contains proven steps and strategies on how to use the power within you to get what you desire in life. Do you want to become rich? Be more powerful? Do you want happiness? The job you dream about? Have more in life?

Life can be better and easier to live upon if you only know how to use the power that is inherent in you. The power of the mind to attract what you want. But of course, it requires a lot from you if you want to change yourself into a "blessing or money magnet." It comes from knowing what you really want in life.

You have to ask yourself and answer honestly the following questions to find out what you want in life. Who am I? What is my purpose on earth? Am I doing what I am supposed to do? Or just going with the flow? Am I happy with what I achieved or can I be more I am today?

The possibilities are great and beyond if you are ready to get out of your comfort zones and get what the Universe offers. You just need to awaken your inner power by clearly focusing on what you want in life and pursue them using with the powerful tool that is within our grasp anytime, anywhere. All you need it is to be positively aware of what you want and apply the most powerful law of the universe to make all your dreams come true faster and better- The Law of Attraction.

Are you ready?

Thanks again for purchasing this book, I hope you enjoy it!

Chapter 1: What Is The Law Of Attraction?

The Law of Attraction is one of the mysterious laws of the Universe which is believed to be behind the great success of the most notable men and women in history. Of course, they all have exceptional talents and abilities plus tons of perseverance to excel in their chosen fields, but the secret of how they attain success, wealth, power and happiness easily over the others is their ability to command the Law of Attraction to work into their lives.

The Law of Attraction is a subtle yet powerful energy constantly working around you. It is active and just waiting for the acknowledgment to align dreams and desires to shape your reality. It can change your needs to abundance. It can help you achieve your goals and ambitions faster that you can imagine. It is the law that gives the desire of your hearts faster and perfectly in tune to your needs. This is the key that can easily open doors of great opportunities, wealth, happiness and love for you. It is a power within your reach.

Understanding the Law of Attraction can open your awareness to the limitless ability of the Universe to supply all your needs. Life can be better than you can ever imagine. There are endless possibilities of what you can do, have, or get from life. There are no restrictions. Everything is free. All you have to do is open your mind and change your thoughts to bring your desires into realities.

Every day you send in the vast Universe and many times you instantly get what you wish for. The most positive thoughts bring the best results while the negative thoughts attract bad results. This knowledge could explain why worrying and thinking the worst possible scenarios bring unfortunate events while thinking positively gives you wonderful moments.

Thoughts are powerful charms to activate the Law of Attraction in your lives. And with this knowledge, you now can shift your thoughts to gain abundance and desires of your hearts. You have in your command the most powerful key to unlock the great favors of the Universe. You are now in charge of your life and you can make it more wonderful. All you need to do is charge and change your thoughts to command the Law of Attraction to work for you and become a human magnet.

Chapter 2: Practice Brain-Training Strategies

The brain is the most complex organ in your body and has control over the others in your body. What makes the brain extra special is the fact that it forms the physical structure associated by the mind. It gives rise to feelings of happiness, sadness, anger, excitement and more. It can create powered thoughts to change the circumstances of your life. Powered thoughts are mental images of your desires which you send out to the Universe with the belief that they will soon manifest in the real world through the Law of Attraction. Sending strong, clear and positive vibrations attract the best possible results.

To successfully practice the Law of Attraction in your life, you need to train your mind by attracting positive energy that will pull the great changes you want for yourself. By practicing brain-training strategies, you can project thought commands with focus and concentration. Techniques like affirmations, goal-setting, visualization and meditation can help develop mind concentration.

- Make a list, or lists, of what you want to achieve in your lifetime. By writing down your goals, we are sending energized thoughts to the Universe. By reading them every day, you are putting them in your subconscious mind, and by thinking about them constantly, you are commanding the positive energy to act on the manifestations of your desires.

- Use powerful affirmations or positive statements to describe a desired situation until it reaches the subconscious level of the mind. By affirming your dreams and wishes, you are rewiring your mind to believe that everything is possible.

- Spend 5 -15 minutes a day thinking about the things you want to do and how you can do them. Create a vivid, mental picture of getting what you want and feel the good feeling that it evokes.

- Practice gratitude for the good and bad things that are happening in your life. Give thanks for the things you are manifesting as if they are already happening because this sets the Law of Attraction in motion.

- Practice manifesting daily. Start with little things that you want to do or have for the day like a cup of delicious coffee, a book you want to read, a walk in the park or a weekend with the family. Saturate yourself with energized thoughts and feel your emotions soar with happiness. Keep doing it until it actually happens.

Chapter 3: The Power Of Mindfulness Meditation

To become in touch with the ability of your mind to create powerful thoughts, you need to cultivate inner calmness and develop the ability to attune to your present experience with acceptance, compassion and patience. Mindfulness is a mental exercise that helps you take control of your own life.

Mindfulness meditation is the western form of mental activity that uses the Buddhist technique called *Vipassana*or Insight Meditation. The primary purpose of this meditation is to become mindful or getting "the intentional, accepting and non-judgmental focus of one's attention on the emotion, thought and sensation occurring in the present moment."

How to do the Mindfulness Meditation?

- First find a place where you can practice meditation without interruption from anybody. Your bedroom is perfect, so relax and find a comfortable spot. You can use a chair and sit with your back straight, or sit cross-legged on the floor.

- Close your eyes. Feel your breathing. Focus your attention on the movements of your abdomen as you inhale and exhale.

- As you focus on the movements, the thoughts will flow into your mind. Do not entertain these thoughts; refocus on your breathing and abdominal movements.

- Practice this meditation for ten minutes a day and you will clearly see what is currently happening in your life and immediate environment. Instead of becoming angry, afraid and worried about it, you will experience a sense of knowing what to do in your present situation. Act on it mentally, fight your problems and overcome them.

- And start using the learned technique to your particular goals to achieve success, prosperity, happiness by focusing on your thought that will attract the blessings of the Divine God.

Chapter 4: Channeling The Subconscious Mind And The Positive Vibrations

Your thoughts are power. They are energy that attracts the same energy. If you want to truly experience the power of the Law of Attraction, you need to consciously train your mind to think differently and powerfully.

Your mind is composed of three realms: the conscious mind or surface consciousness where you are aware of your thoughts, intentions, feelings and actions; the subconscious mind where thoughts, beliefs and mental processes go beneath the conscious mind; and finally, the subtle energetic mind where the Law of Attraction works.

Your conscious mind is responsible for your reasoning, logic, calculations and actions or performances.

While subconscious mind stores your experiences, your bitter-sweet memories and responsible for the instant emotion or feeling you manifest upon facing a new or similar situation.

You are who you think you are. So think positively and send positive vibrations in the Universe in order to attract positive energy back to you. The stronger the vibrations you send out, the more favors you will receive from the universe. People and circumstances are adjusting into your life to create the positive manifestations of your desires and goals.

Pay attention to your vivid dreams. They can relay messages from your subconscious mind to help you in the current situation you are facing. You can reflect on them and pay attention to the details of your dreams to unlock their hidden meaning.

Listen also to your intuition, this is another subconscious awareness that you need to heed the wisdom especially during times of confusion and chaos. If you feel something is not right about a particular person or situation, you need to listen to this inner voice to avoid tragedy or further problems.

Play the guessing game to develop your subconscious mind. Tune into your intuition and make predictions of what will happen in the next few hours. This exciting game will let you exercise your mental abilities. Try guessing who is calling you without looking at your phone, or make a guess about who is knocking on your front door before you open it.

And finally trust your subconscious mind by filling it with positive vibrations and your life can have a complete transformation.

Chapter 5: How To Use Creative Visualization

Creative visualization is a mental activity which is used to manifest what you desire much faster. It is a technique where you use your imagination to create a clear picture of what you want to have or what you want to become in the near future. By changing your thoughts positively and getting in tune with your desires, you can change the physical plane of your life.

One of the most read success books that talked about the creative visualization is "The Science of Getting Rich" by Wallace Wattles. According to him, everything evolved from thoughts. Whatever you consistently think about will expand and materialize in your life.

Creative visualization is one of the secrets of people who gain recognition especially athletes and performers. They do it by focusing on the finish line or the end of the production and the positive thoughts give them the energy to move forward and perform their best. Celebrities like Oprah, Will Smith, Drew Barrymore and Jim Carrey confessed that they use creative visualization many times to help them overcome challenges.

Creative visualization is the mental preparation of the actual happening or event, so be sure that you prepare for it just as you would in actual experience.

For instance, you want to win a singing competition, so you practice your favorite song repeatedly until you start to get sick of hearing yourself sing. While you are taking a break from practice, try using creative visualization to prepare yourself further before going to the competition. You focus on the thought that the host called your name, you climb on stage, you perform the song with all the emotions you have in your heart, you can see the audience listening intently and appreciating your performance. Now you see them clapping, the judges beaming and the host announced that you are the champion! You feel really good! And you feel more ready to break a leg! That is how creative visualization works. If you find obstacles along the way to your desire, imagine yourself doing something to resolve it at once so that you will emerge a winner. Do it again until you can feel in your heart that you are truly a winner. So that when you do the actual thing, you will be better prepared to perform and win the top prize.

The Law of Attraction is available to all of us anytime anywhere. You just need to form a mental thought picture of your goals by this creative visualization and see all your dreams unfold and come true.

Chapter 6: How To Manifest Money And Wealth By Law Of Attraction

Who does not want to be wealthy and travel around the world? Who does not want to have a comfortable life without stress brought about by financial constraints? Who does not want to have more than what they need?

You can manifest money and wealth by using the Law of Attraction.

- First, always be positive. This is one of the basic key to attract the positive things you want to have. Being positive means keeping the faith that what you prayed for is on the way. Being positive means living as if the answer is in your hands

- Second, to improve your current financial status, you need to improve your money vibe. It means you do not focus on the absence of money but of the abundance. If you keep seeing your money depleting, and you are constantly worrying about it, then you are magnifying your needs and your lack of money. However, if you can shift your thoughts and consider the situation as just a momentary thing, and you believe that money will come rushing into your pockets, then your money vibe will improve. You will become more energetic and inspired to find alternative means to earn while waiting for the windfall.

- If you want money-don't worry. Do the opposite. Imagine having more money, more than you can count at once. Imagine spending it and buying everything that you want. Imagine paying off all of your debts. Imagine giving money to your family and friends. Feel the good feelings by just imagining that you have that amount of money. It feels better than worrying yourself to death because you do not have the money.

- Be thankful of what remains in your wallets or bank account. Appreciate the fact that you still have money to buy food or pay the bills. Appreciating what you have right now is sending a positive signal to the universe that you are thanking God for what you receive and you will be given more.

Chapter 7: Happiness And Law Of Attraction

Happiness is personal thing. It is a feeling of fulfillment or satisfaction that you have in your hearts from the things you do, the persons you care about, the decisions you make and the achievements you gain along the way.

And your thoughts are the main factors why you perceive happiness. If you expect happiness, you will receive happiness. This is how the Law of Attraction works in your life. If you expect loneliness then it will happen. So be sure that what you are sending out in the Universe is a positive feeling that will make you happy not sad. As I said, happiness is a personal thing. The things that make you happy are different from mine. But one thing is constant-your thoughts.

Who says that happiness is an elusive feeling?

Happiness is within your grasp. All you have to do is to know what makes you happy. Is it your job, family, realization of your goals, money, love? Getting what you desire makes you feel satisfied and happy. And the intensity of happiness depends upon the degree of satisfaction you experienced.

In the Law of Attraction where thoughts are the most essential factor of getting what you want to get, you need to think consistently about what brings you happiness. It may come upon the things you are doing in your life right now or the simple act of sharing your talents, resources and time. Thinking about them over and over again is applying the Law of Attraction.

By constant thinking of those thoughts that brings smile to your lips, peaceful joy in your hearts you are sending happy vibrations in the universe. It creates impact, resounding on the different corners of the cosmos plane and sending back positive vibrations to you.

So if you want to attain happiness in different aspects of your life or you are in the journey to happiness, remember it is all in your mind. The secret is consistently thinking your goals with focus. Make it a habit to think about them, feel them come true, feel that you have them now, be happy and happiness will embrace you. If other emotions come in as you take your journey in your mind, set them aside or solve them mentally and get back to your train of happy thoughts.

So practice. Make it a habit. Train your mind to think about what gives you happiness. Until such time that it comes naturally and unconsciously seeping into your perceptions. Happy thoughts gives happy feelings that you need to be reminded that what you are doing are essential to your well-being.

Chapter 8: Finding Love With Law Of Attraction

Looking for love? Are you searching for that special person who will make your world insanely happy? With the Law of Attraction, you can definitely attract that person, heal your relationships, or make your ex come back to you.

However, finding love with the Law of Attraction is not all about switching your mind to the person you want to have in your life.

You need to focus first on yourself first. Are you ready for a serious relationship? Are you ready for commitment? Are you ready to find happiness with him or her? You need to feel it, to desire it, to attune yourself to the feeling of love, of being with the special man or woman to share your happiness and your future.

You need to love yourself first. Make yourself happy being you before you can love another person. By knowing your wants and needs and fulfilling them, you are unconsciously preparing to expand your capacity to love; you cannot share what you do not have. If your life is full of love, you are ready to take additional steps to find happiness by loving.

Feel great by knowing yourself. Be confident that you have the qualities that are irresistible and worth loving.

The Law of Attraction dictates that you need to desire something with all your heart. Focus on that feeling. Think about that special someone and how nice to be around her or him. Acknowledge the happy feeling when you are with him or her.

Do not be afraid of the emotions that will come if you open your heart by loving this special person. Be confident that you can overcome the tests and trials of a relationship. You know you can handle them because you have mentally rehearsed every step towards the goal of making this special person a part of your life.

Attune your feelings, your thoughts, your actions, and your happiness to the positive vibrations you send out constantly to the universe and feel the results of using this Law of Attraction.

Of course, let the person know your intention and start the ball rolling and continue shape your thoughts to attain your ultimate goal of making this person keep you in his heart and life.

Chapter 9: Steps In Using Law Of Attraction In Daily Life

We all have the key to everything that we desire in our hands. The most important thing is to continue practicing the Law of Attraction to attract the affirmative things in your life. The Law is a powerful tool that we can constantly use to have a quality life, find the perfect job, find the love of your life, enhance personal relationships, the wealth you want to acquire, the happiness you crave, and practically everything else you desire.

For the Law of Attraction to work, you need to make it habit and practice it every day. You have the power within you. You only have to unleash the belief that you can have it. Live with the knowledge of knowing you deserve to have the kind of life you desire not only for your own benefit but for the people around you.

Use the brain-training strategies discussed earlier.

Meditate and center your focus on the thoughts that will make a big difference between success and failure.

Practice the habit of creative visualization to create changes, to restore, to heal, to begin and to achieve.

Make the mysterious Law of Attraction a part of your daily dealings by preparing yourself, your important presentations, your plans and your actions for the day, and attract the blessings you want to have.

You can also become a better person as you along the process of altering your whole life by using the Law of Attraction. Become the best and you will receive the best. It is the law of the universe. Sow what you want and reap what you want.

Chapter 10: Dreaming Big With Law Of Attraction

Now that you have all the necessary knowledge, you can dream BIG and achieve what you desire faster. You only need to continue your daily task, enjoying the journey of living and appreciating the outcomes, regardless of whether they are good or bad. You know you can have more of life's blessings, because in your hands is the power to gain abundance in all aspects of your life.   So act now. Aim high and dream big, and the universe will give you what you need, especially if your desires are in line with your purpose of being here on earth.

Go for it, do your best, control your mind, use the law of Attraction and wait as the best results unfold. Do not forget to show your gratitude. All you have to do is ask positively with focused thoughts consistently and let the Law of Attraction work for you.

Conclusion

Thank you again for purchasing this book on how to use the Law of Attraction!

I am extremely excited to pass this information along to you, and I am so happy that you now have read and can hopefully implement these strategies going forward.

I hope this book was able to help you understand the Law Of Attraction and how to use it to attain abundance in your life and everything that makes your life better if not the best.

The next step is to get started using this information and to hopefully live a happy, fulfilling and meaningful life!

Please don't be someone who just reads this information and doesn't apply it, the strategies in this book will only benefit you if you use them!

If you know of anyone else that could benefit from the information presented here please inform them of this book.

Finally, if you enjoyed this book and feel it has added value to your life in any way, please take the time to share your thoughts and post a review on Amazon. It'd be greatly appreciated!

Thank you and good luck!

Preview Of:

Ultimate Manifestation Guide!

Manifestation

The Science Of Manifestation Through Neuroplasticity, Brain Training, NLP Techniques, Creative Visualization, Mindfulness Meditation, And More!

Introduction

I want to thank you and congratulate you for purchasing the book, *"Manifestation: Ultimate Manifestation Guide! The Science Of Manifestation Through Neuroplasticity, Brain Training, NLP Techniques, Creative Visualization, Mindfulness Meditation, And More!"*

This book contains proven steps and strategies on how to use manifestation techniques to attract the things that you want in life. This book will help you understand the universal law of attraction and help you use it to transform your dreams into reality.

If you feel that your life is getting nowhere and you feel that you cannot control the outcome of your life, this book is for you. This book will help you understand the power of your mind to change your life for the better. This book will also help you realize that you are the master of your life and you have the creative power to map out your destiny.

Thanks again for purchasing this book, I hope you enjoy it!

Chapter 1 - Proof That Manifestation Is Real

The law of attraction is quite popular nowadays. Many celebrities believe it and many claim that they have used it to achieve success and personal transformation. But is it really real?

Well, the law of attraction is a universal law that states that the more you think about something, the more it manifests in your life. So, if you think about success often, if you believe that you are destined for success, you will eventually achieve success. If you think about failure, on the other hand, you will attract people and circumstances that will orchestrate to deliver what you expect – failure.

Have you noticed that whenever you think about a person that you have not thought about for years, he suddenly shows up days later? Have you noticed that if you express interest on, say, traveling to Paris, you will begin to see airline ads and deals that would help you realize your Paris dream vacation? That's huge proof that the law of manifestation is real.

To further illustrate this point, let's take a look at the success stories of celebrities who have deliberately used the law of attraction to bring success into their lives. In the 1980s, Jim Carrey was a struggling actor. He was constantly depressed and he has a hard time trying to make ends meet. He has read about the law of attraction and he decided to give it a try. He wrote himself a check worth ten million dollars and dated the check 1995. He kept the check in his wallet for years. He had nearly forgotten about it. In 1994, Jim Carrey got his breakout roles as Ace Ventura: The Pet Detective and as The Mask. Because of the success of these two films, his market value have significantly increased and he received a ten million dollar check in 1994 for his acting service in the film "Dumb and Dumber".

In 1985, Oprah Winfrey read the book called "The Color Purple". She never stopped thinking about the book and she was literally addicted to it. Years later, her agent called and said that she got an audition for the movie adaptation of "The Color Purple". She wanted the part so bad that she regularly prayed for it. She visualized herself going to the set and shooting the film. She waited for the callback for months and finally, she got the part. Oprah said that the fact that she wanted the part so bad and she believed that she can achieve it and that she is worthy of it is the starting point of her successful career.

The power of thought to influence manifestation was also proven by the water experiment conducted by Dr. Emoto Masaru. Dr. Masaru and his team studies the molecular structure of normal water when frozen. They then asked a monk to bless a glass of water with gratitude and love. They froze the water and they were surprised to see that the molecular structure of the water that was blessed by the monk is different from the unblessed water. The water that was exposed to feelings of love, gratitude, and peace have a beautiful flower-like molecular structure. They then exposed another glass of water to music that is full of angst and hatred. They were also shock to find out that the water exposed to anger have a distorted and ugly molecular form.

The result of this experiment is proof that our thoughts and emotions influence our outer or physical reality. Remember that our body and the world are mainly made of water. Notice that if you wake up in the morning feeling cranky, you will attract negative circumstances because you have emitted negative vibes. If you wake up thinking that it is going to be a bad day, well, it is definitely going to be a bad day. The universe will deliver whatever you expect.

The law of attraction is real and it has helped many people achieve the life that they have always dreamed of. Now is the time for you to use it to your advantage and achieve everything that you have hoped for.

Thanks for Previewing My Exciting Book Entitled:

"Manifestation: Ultimate Manifestation Guide! The Science Of Manifestation Through Neuroplasticity, Brain Training, NLP Techniques, Creative Visualization, Mindfulness Meditation, And More!"

To purchase this book, simply go to the Amazon Kindle store and simply search:

"MANIFESTATION"

Then just scroll down until you see my book. You will know it is mine because you will see my name "Ryan Cooper" underneath the title.

Alternatively, you can visit my author page on Amazon to see this book and other work I have done. Thanks so much, and please don't forget your free bonuses

DON'T LEAVE YET! - CHECK OUT YOUR FREE BONUSES BELOW!

Free Bonus Offer 1: Get Free Access To The <u>OperationAwesomeLife.com</u> VIP Newsletter!

Free Bonus Offer 2: Get A Free Download Of My Friends Amazing Book "Passive Income" First Chapter!

Free Bonus Offer 3: Get A Free Email Series On Making Money Online When You Join Newsletter!

GET ALL 3 FREE

Once you enter your email address you will immediately get free access to this awesome **VIP NEWSLETTER!**

For a limited time, if you join for free right now, you will also get free access to the first chapter of the awesome book **"PASSIVE INCOME"!**

And, last but definitely not least, if you join the newsletter right now, you also will get a free 10 part email series on **10 SUCCESS SECRETS OF MAKING MONEY ONLINE!**

To claim all 3 of your FREE BONUSES just click below!

<u>Just Go Here for all 3 VIP bonuses!</u>

OperationAwesomeLife.com

Printed in Great Britain
by Amazon.co.uk, Ltd.,
Marston Gate.